# Poems!

Matthew Long

Presentation by *BookLeaf Publishing*

Web: www.bookleafpub.com

E-mail: info@bookleafpub.com


ISBN: 9789357616096

First edition 2022

# Beginning

Is Easy.
Knowing where to go
Is the hard part.

# I have not been outside today


It could all be gone for all I know.
I've stayed inside, kept my windows closed.
Turned the stereo on
89.5 CIUT on the radio.
You are here still,
On the couch;
Where else would I go?

# Fan Haiku

Fan swivels it's head
Blowing air through the basement
White noise helps to sleep.

# I felt happy

Driving home from Fortinos
A few weeks ago,
A spontaneous smile
Crossed my face.
No music on the radio.
Oakwood not busy with traffic.
Fall colours beginning to fill into the leaves.
I arrived home,
Then received a text message that
Stressed me out.
It didn't last long,
But I did feel happy.

# It all changed

After that rainy Sunday
Cleaning my bedroom
Listening to Blue Rodeo 5 Days in July,
Steve Miller's Greatest Hits,
and The Beatles 1.

# Old Man for the first time

I listened to Neil Young's Old Man
For the first time in my memory
Early one morning
After downloading it off Limewire.

You were awake.
I went downstairs to ask
If you knew the song.
You said yes.
I asked what was wrong.
You said Steve died.
Your Steve or Mom's? I asked.
Mine, you said.
I said i'm sorry.
I hope I hugged you.
Then I went upstairs
And played the Sims.

# Apples

We went apple picking.
What will I do
With all these apples?
Keep eating apples?

# How much


Do we really need?
Isn't there enough?

# Gah

It carries on
Relentlessly.

# 2022

Has been an unusual year
And
It's not over yet.

# I watched

Beauty and the Beast
Over and Over
For like, a year
As a young child.

# I miss you


And think about you
Often.

# X-Files

Not long after we first moved to Ontario,
We went as a family to the Ex.
There was a large bunker
Full of merchandise for us to buy
And I remember finding these spooky
X-Files toys with Mulder and Scully models
On the sets of some alien scene.
Watching Mulder and Scully on TV
As a young boy
Was confusing back then.
Why did I find
Both of them to be attractive?
I wanted the toys
But we could not afford them.
I was too young to watch the show regularly.
But Mulder and Scully haven't gone anywhere.
I'm less confused now, at least.

# All this stuff

Haunts me more than it helps me;
Reminding me of all I have not done
When I choose to do
Something new.
I am working through it, though.
Selling what I don't need,
Donating some too,
Reading the books,
Watching the movies I've always wanted to
watch.
I listened to all my records
Through the pandemic.
Slowly, the pressure
Has begun to dissipate.

# I don't expect much

But it better work out
How I want it to.

# I still remember

Each of your suggestions
For books to write
Such as
When I Was Six
And
Building Sheds and Mending Relationships.

I still remember
Your plan to make a photo book
Of the dilapidated barns along Dundas
Before they were torn down for destruction.

You taught me about music
And taught how to drive.
I always think of you
Blasting I Want You
From Abbey Road
As we drove down the dark winding
Trafalgar road.
You showed me how to be a good man.
You're always there when I need you.
Always wanting me to take it easy
And do what I need to do,
Like you did,
Working the hard jobs

Working nights and driving us to school after.
Always doing what you needed to do.

You're my hero
for so many reasons.
Thank you.

# West Side Avenue (From 2008)

An Italian madman stood at the front of the
crowd.
He shouted his desires for he could explain them
now.
No one can hear you bitch if you're being too
loud.
You got to get them in and teach them or throw
them out.
The beat up poets smoked as they recorded
every thought.
Stream of conscious musings to make fortunes
off of.
There was fodder here, enough for two
best-selling books.
Even if no one gets it, they know its genius they
got into.

Seventeen suitors swept through the streets.
Their faces were close but their feet would never
meet.
Years had passed but they didn't know each
other's names.
It wasn't important; it wasn't part of the game.

Inexhaustible soldiers filtered through the floors.
They were faced with decisions; it felt like a
new war.
Even when you take a break, the fight keeps on
coming.
They never know their enemies but they know
they're worth gunning.

Tangents of monsters crawled up the walls.
They've got to escape the government; they're
all hoping they'll fall.
But these city officials never realize they got
their tricks
How else have they survived while needing their
kicks?

Solitary men wore coats with slogans they didn't
get.
They could dance and cheer but they'd rather
brood, I bet.
It wasn't fair to assume that they could let their
feelings out.
But I wouldn't be surprised if that's what they
want to do right now.

There were waves of men who wont breathe
without being told.
They wanted to stand by the side since
spectacles never get old.

If they could get through this, they know this
will help their mind grow.
But so many things can stop you, that's one
thing even they know.

Every man you ever met saw you walking alone.
They were holding their babies and their wives
were on thrones.
They can see that you're sick but they can't stop.
They gave you their time before despite what
you thought.

West Side Avenue is leaking with people.
They're all going to take a break when they get
to Mary's steeple.
These colorful figures need help as they
relentlessly walk.
But too many things are stopping them from
living, and they can't talk.

I saw everyone as they kept moving on.
I can't remember them all, but their impressions
were strong.
I won't stay here unless this movement needs
support.
But at least I can always say that I was there that
day.

West Side Avenue is leaking with fearless folks.

They can't stop until they know it is not a hoax.
There's certainly a chance that they will get a
break.
But there is no doubt, we'll all need to wait.

# Not all of us are so lucky to have known all of you

Kim
David
Michael
April
Isabelle
Jocelyne
Robert
Mary
Lisita
Greg
Alex
Phil
Vicky
Ruby
Oliver
Josh
Alison
Beatrix
Mark
Jordan
Doneva
Shaun
Liam